SHAR

Catholic Social

Teaching

CHALLENGES AND
DIRECTIONS

REFLECTIONS OF THE U.S. CATHOLIC BISHOPS

Revised Edition

ALSO INCLUDES THE SUMMARY REPORT
OF THE TASK FORCE ON
CATHOLIC SOCIAL TEACHING AND
CATHOLIC EDUCATION

UNITED STATES CONFERENCE OF CATHOLIC BISHOPS
WASHINGTON, D.C.

This publication contains two documents—the bishops' statement *Sharing Catholic Social Teaching: Challenges and Directions* and the *Summary Report of the Task Force on Catholic Social Teaching and Catholic Education*. The bishops' statement was developed by the Committee on Education, the Committee on Domestic Policy, and the Committee on International Policy, and it was approved by the bishops on June 19, 1998. It is a response to the report of the Task Force on Catholic Social Teaching and Catholic Education, which was created in 1995 by these three committees. The task force's summary report is included as an appendix to this publication. The bishops' statement reflects the action of the bishops, and the summary report is the work of the task force. These two documents are approved for publication by the undersigned.

> *Monsignor Dennis M. Schnurr*
> *General Secretary*
> NCCB/USCC

In 2001 the National Conference of Catholic Bishops (NCCB) and the United States Catholic Conference (USCC) became the United States Conference of Catholic Bishops (USCCB).

Scripture texts used in this work are taken from the *New American Bible*, copyright © 1991, 1986, and 1970 by the Confraternity of Christian Doctrine, Washington, DC 20017 and are used by permission of the copyright owner. All rights reserved.

First Printing, June 1998
First Printing, Revised Edition, August 2009

ISBN 978-1-60137-085-3

Contents

There are many innovative efforts by Catholic educators to communicate the social doctrine of the Church. At the same time, however, it is clear that in some educational programs Catholic social teaching is not really shared or not sufficiently integral and explicit. As a result, far too many Catholics are not familiar with the basic content of Catholic social teaching. More fundamentally, many Catholics do not adequately understand that the social teaching of the Church is an essential part of Catholic faith. This poses a serious challenge for all Catholics, since it weakens our capacity to be a Church that is true to the demands of the Gospel.

SHARING

Catholic Social Teaching

CHALLENGES AND DIRECTIONS

REFLECTIONS OF THE U.S. CATHOLIC BISHOPS

Introduction

Our community of faith is blessed with many gifts. Two of the most vital are our remarkable commitment to Catholic education and catechesis in all its forms and our rich tradition of Catholic social teaching. As we look to a new millennium, there is an urgent need to bring these two gifts together in a strengthened commitment to sharing our social teaching at every level of Catholic education and faith formation.

Catholic social teaching is a central and essential element of our faith. Its roots are in the Hebrew Prophets who announced God's special love for the poor and called God's people to a covenant of love and justice. It is a teaching founded on the life and words of Jesus Christ, who came "to bring glad tidings to the poor / . . . liberty to captives / . . . recovery of sight to the blind" (Lk 4:18-19), and who identified himself with "the least of these," the hungry and the stranger (cf. Mt 25:45). Catholic social teaching is built on a commitment to the poor. This commitment arises

CATHOLIC JUSTICE EDUCATOR'S NETWORK

The Catholic Justice Educator's Network (CJEN) in the Archdiocese of St. Paul and Minneapolis gives teachers and catechists in Catholic schools, religious education programs, and youth ministry groups a chance to share ways to infuse social justice into various educational settings. A joint effort between the archdiocesan Catholic Education and Formation Ministries and the Office for Social Justice, the network produces a newsletter three times a year in which teachers share ideas, lesson plans, and experiences. This information is also available on the Internet at *www.osjspm.org*. For more information, contact the Office for Social Justice at (651) 291-4477.

from our experiences of Christ in the Eucharist. As the *Catechism of the Catholic Church* explains, "To receive in truth the Body and Blood of Christ given up for us, we must recognize Christ in the poorest, his brethren" (no. 1397).

Catholic social teaching emerges from the truth of what God has revealed to us about himself. We believe in the triune God whose very nature is communal and social. God the Father sends his only Son Jesus Christ and shares the Holy Spirit as his gift of love. God reveals himself to us as one who is not alone, but rather as one who is relational, one who is Trinity. Therefore, we who are made in God's image share this communal, social nature. We are called to reach out and to build relationships of love and justice.

Catholic social teaching is based on and inseparable from our understanding of human life and human dignity. Every human being is created in the image of God and redeemed by Jesus Christ, and therefore is invaluable and worthy of respect as a member of the human family. Every person, from the moment of conception to natural death, has inherent dignity and a right to life consistent with that dignity. Human dignity comes from God, not from any human quality or accomplishment.

Our commitment to the Catholic social mission must be rooted in and strengthened by our spiri-

INTERNATIONAL DAYS

Several hundred seventh-grade student leaders from the Archdiocese of Seattle participate in an annual "International Day," a leadership program coordinated by the Archdiocesan Schools Department with support from the archdiocesan offices for Catholic Relief Services and Propagation of the Faith. Each year an international peace and justice theme is chosen for the International Day. Over the years students have addressed such problems as conflicts in the Middle East and in Guatemala. For 1998, the theme was stewardship of the earth, and students focused on the international discord that has arisen in response to the U.N.'s attempt to reduce individual countries' greenhouse gas emissions. Local teachers, missioners, and other overseas volunteers facilitate additional activities and lectures that enhance the students' awareness of international issues and the universal Church's social mission. Former participants are highly enthusiastic about the experience and claim it has a lasting impact on their attention to international social justice issues. For information, contact the Catholic Schools Office, Archdiocese of Seattle, at (206) 382-4861.

tual lives. In our relationship with God we experience the conversion of heart that is necessary to truly love one another as God has loved us.

A Time to Act

Because this commitment to social justice is at the heart of who we are and what we believe, it must be shared more effectively. We offer these reflections to address the pressing need to educate all Catholics on the Church's social teaching and to share the social demands of the Gospel and Catholic tradition more clearly. If Catholic education and formation fail to communicate our social tradition, they are not fully Catholic.

This statement is addressed in a particular way to those engaged in Catholic education, catechesis, and social ministry. As pastors and as teachers of the faith, we ask Catholic educators and catechists to join with us in facing the urgent challenge of communicating Catholic social teaching more fully to all the members of our family of faith.

This is a call to action, an appeal especially to pastors, educators, and catechists to teach the Catholic social tradition in its fullness. These reflections are not a comprehensive summary

YOUTH GROUPS AND PEACEMAKING

The Office of Peace and Justice of the Diocese of Raleigh, North Carolina, provides trained facilitators to help youth groups throughout the diocese study Catholic teaching on peace and justice. Materials on peace and justice issues that are specifically designed for young people are also provided. The youth groups are then encouraged to participate in local organizations funded by the Catholic Campaign for Human Development. The diocese provides small grants to help cover transportation and other costs. For more information, call the Office of Peace and Justice at (704) 370-3225.

of its rich heritage and content. Our social tradition has been developed and expressed through a variety of major documents, including papal encyclicals, conciliar documents, and episcopal statements. The *Catechism of the Catholic Church* summarizes the essence of this social teaching and roots it in faith and liturgical life, presenting it as an essential part of the moral teaching of the Church. In addition, the Vatican has developed *Guidelines for the Study and Teaching of the*

Church's Social Doctrine in the Formation of Priests. Our own conference of bishops has outlined this heritage in *A Century of Social Teaching*. Catholic social teaching can be understood best through a thorough study of papal teaching and ecclesial documents.

The focus of this statement is the urgent task to incorporate Catholic social teaching more fully and explicitly into Catholic educational programs. This must be undertaken in the context of efforts to share the faith in its entirety and to encourage Catholics to experience the gospel call to conversion in all its dimensions. Recognizing the importance of this broader goal of Catholic education and formation, we call for a renewed commitment to integrate Catholic social teaching into the mainstream of all Catholic educational institutions and programs. We are confident that this goal can be advanced, because we know firsthand of the dedication, talent, and deep faith of those involved in the work of education, catechesis, and faith formation. The work done by principals, teachers, catechists, directors and coordinators of religious education, youth ministers, college and seminary professors, adult educators, and social action leaders is vitally important. We thank and commend all those who carry out the holy work of educating others to understand and to act on the truths of our faith. We recognize the commitment and creativity of so many educators and catechists who already share our social tradition in their classrooms and programs.

However, despite these significant and ongoing efforts, our social heritage is unknown by many Catholics. Sadly, our social doctrine is not shared or taught in a consistent and comprehensive way in too many of our schools, seminaries, religious education programs, colleges, and universities. We need to build on the good work already underway to ensure that every Catholic understands how the Gospel and church teaching call us to choose life, to serve the least among us, to hunger and thirst for justice, and to be peacemakers. The sharing of our social tradition is a defining measure of Catholic education and formation.

The Task Force's Mission and Findings

For these reasons, in 1995 our bishops' conference established the Task Force on Catholic Social Teaching and Catholic Education. The task force brought leaders of Catholic education and social ministry together to assess and strengthen current efforts and to develop new directions for the future.

As Catholic bishops in the United States we have received and very much welcome the report of the Task Force on Catholic Social Teaching and Catholic Education. We affirm their work and urge action on their report. Our brief reflections here do not take the place of the full report, but we wish to highlight several key themes developed by the task force. After our reflections, you will also find the task force summary report.

In its overall assessment, the task force found much good will

SWEATSHOPS AND FAIR LABOR PRACTICES

An initiative to educate principals, teachers, and students about the injustices of sweatshops has been launched by the Archdiocese of Newark. An initial consumer action program identified manufacturers of Catholic school uniforms sold in the archdiocese, determined compliance with labor laws, and informed school principals of the status of such companies. The program asked manufacturers and suppliers to conform to fair labor standards. In conjunction with the consumer action, schools in the archdiocese were supplied with a learning module to teach students in grades seven through twelve about labor issues and the injustice of sweatshops.

"Catholic social teaching has stressed always the dignity of every human being," explained Cardinal Theodore McCarrick, former Archbishop of Newark. "We believe that everyone has the right to have their basic human needs for food, clothing, health care, and housing met through just wages and safe working conditions. We believe we have an obligation to teach those principles to the students in our schools and in our religious education programs."

and many innovative efforts by Catholic educators to communicate the social doctrine of the Church. At the same time, however, it is clear that in some educational programs Catholic social teaching is not really shared or not sufficiently integral and explicit. As a result, far too many Catholics are not familiar with the basic content of Catholic social teaching. More fundamentally, many Catholics do not adequately understand that the social teaching of the Church is an essential part of Catholic faith. This poses a serious challenge for all Catholics, since it weakens our capacity to be a Church that is true to the demands of the Gospel. We need to do more to share the social mission and message of our Church.

Our Catholic social teaching is proclaimed whenever we gather for worship. The homily presents an excellent opportunity for sharing Catholic social teaching. The word of God announces God's reign of justice and peace. Our preaching of the just word continues the preaching of Jesus and the Prophets.

Central to our identity as Catholics is that we are called to be leaven for transforming the world, agents for bringing about a kingdom of love and justice. When we pray, "Thy kingdom come; thy will be done on earth as it is in heaven," we are praying for God's

"WRITE MAKES MIGHT"
Seventh graders at St. Genevieve School in Thibodaux, Louisiana, learned about the importance of bringing the principles of Catholic social teaching to the political process when they produced a booklet titled *Write Makes Might*. The booklet explains the importance of participating in legislative activity and offers a practical guide for writing to members of the state and national legislature. According to principal Caroline Cappel, "I have heard of several former students who, as young adults, have taken their concern for social justice issues beyond the confines of our community. I think this project helped." For information, contact St. Genevieve School at (985) 447-9883.

kingdom of justice and peace and committing ourselves to breaking down the barriers that obstruct God's kingdom of justice and peace and to working to bring about a world more respectful of human life and dignity.

Catholic Social Teaching: Major Themes

The Church's social teaching is a rich treasure of wisdom about building a just society and living lives of holiness amidst the challenges of modern society. It offers moral principles and coherent values that are badly needed in our time. In this time of widespread violence and diminished respect for human life and dignity in our country and around the world, the Gospel of life and the biblical call to justice need to be proclaimed and shared with new clarity, urgency, and energy.

Modern Catholic social teaching has been articulated through a tradition of papal, conciliar, and episcopal documents that explore and express the social demands of our faith. The depth and richness of this tradition can be understood best through a direct reading of these documents, many of which are cited in the Report of the Content Subgroup (pp. 32-42). In these brief reflections, we wish to highlight several of the key themes that are at the heart of our Catholic social tradition. We hope they will serve as a starting point for those interested in exploring the Catholic social tradition more fully.

Life and Dignity of the Human Person

In a world warped by materialism and declining respect for human life, the Catholic Church proclaims that human life is sacred

"BEING THERE"

Elementary school teachers in the Diocese of Kansas City–St. Joseph, Missouri, can participate in Being There, an immersion program sponsored by the diocesan Peace and Justice Office. The program is designed to give faculties direct experience with people living in poverty and to deepen their understanding of the Church's "preferential option for the poor." One faculty at a time participates by spending a day visiting programs in low-income neighborhoods such as food kitchens, literacy programs, child care facilities, and congregation-based organizing projects. Time for reflection and discussion are incorporated throughout the day and are an essential component of the experience.

The diocesan Peace and Justice Office also sponsors adult education programs focused on the principles of Catholic social teaching. Sessions are held in parishes and include such topics as "Human Dignity," "The Common Good," and "The Dignity and Rights of Workers." For more information, contact the Office of Human Rights, Diocese of Kansas City–St. Joseph, at (816) 324-3179.

and that the dignity of the human person is the foundation of a moral vision for society. Our belief in the sanctity of human life and the inherent dignity of the human person is the foundation of all the principles of our social teaching. In our society, human life is under direct attack from abortion and assisted suicide. The value of human life is being threatened by increasing use of the death penalty. The dignity of life is undermined when the creation of human life is reduced to the manufacture of a product, as in human cloning or proposals for genetic engineering to create "perfect" human beings. We believe that every person is precious, that people are more important than things, and that the measure of every institution is whether it threatens or enhances the life and dignity of the human person.

Call to Family, Community, and Participation

In a global culture driven by excessive individualism, our tradition proclaims that the person is not only sacred but also social. How we organize our society—in economics and politics, in law and policy—directly affects human dignity and the capacity of individuals to grow in community. The family is the central social institution that must be supported and

---

UNIVERSITY OF ST. THOMAS
The University of St. Thomas in St. Paul, Minnesota, offers a variety of programs focused on the Catholic social tradition. The university's Center for Catholic Studies offers courses on Catholic social thought that are integrated into undergraduate and graduate level programs. The center also sponsors the Institute for Christian Social Thought and Management, which focuses on the significance of Catholic social thought for business, as well as the Focus on Theology Program, a set of written and audiovisual resources designed to give teachers in Catholic elementary schools, secondary schools, and religious education programs an opportunity to reflect on Catholic social principles. Regular faculty development seminars help connect Catholic social teaching to a variety of disciplines.

The university has made a commitment to take a leadership role in responding to the Task Force on Catholic Social Teaching and Catholic Education. The Center for Catholic Studies plans to establish an Institute for Catholic Social Teaching and Catholic Education, which will help implement the recommendations of the task force. For information, contact the Center for Catholic Studies at (651) 962-5700 or cathstudies@stthomas.edu.

strengthened, not undermined. While our society often exalts individualism, the Catholic tradition teaches that human beings grow and achieve fulfillment in community. We believe people have a right and a duty to participate in society, seeking together the common good and well-being of all, especially the poor and vulnerable. Our Church teaches that the role of government and other institutions is to protect human life and human dignity and promote the common good.

Rights and Responsibilities

In a world where some speak mostly of "rights" and others mostly of "responsibilities," the Catholic tradition teaches that human dignity can be protected and a healthy community can be achieved only if human rights are protected and responsibilities are met. Therefore, every person has a fundamental right to life and a right to those things required for human decency. Corresponding to these rights are duties and responsibilities—to one another, to our families, and to the larger society. While public

NATIONAL ISSUES FORUMS IN THE CATHOLIC COMMUNITY

Vatican II challenged Catholic Christians to connect faith and life. One of the ways adults do that is in their life roles—as parent, spouse, worker, and citizen.

National Issues Forums in the Catholic Community (NIFCC) is an adult education resource that empowers Catholics to be more effective citizens. It is the result of a partnership between the Kettering Foundation and the USCC Department of Education.

NIFCC utilizes the "town meeting"— one of the oldest practices of our young democracy—as its primary strength. The format encourages people to gather in a public place to search together for solutions to such urgent domestic issues as the environment, health care, gambling, family values, race relations, and governance. A Catholic supplement, written especially for each issue, sheds the light of our Church's rich social teaching on the deliberation.

NIFCC is a fresh way to talk about domestic issues. The materials and the process ensure that the deliberation will be inclusive, respectful, non-partisan, and illuminated by reliable sources of information. Forums lead to public knowledge, common ground for action, and later, publicly supportable actions. For further information contact your diocesan Office for Adult Religious Education.

debate in our nation is often divided between those who focus on personal responsibility and those who focus on social responsibilities, our tradition insists that both are necessary.

Option for the Poor and Vulnerable

In a world characterized by growing prosperity for some and pervasive poverty for others, Catholic teaching proclaims that a basic moral test is how our most vulnerable members are faring. In a society marred by deepening divisions between rich and poor, our tradition recalls the story of the Last Judgment (Mt 25:31-46) and instructs us to put the needs of the poor and vulnerable first.

The Dignity of Work and the Rights of Workers

In a marketplace where too often the quarterly bottom line takes precedence over the rights of workers, we believe that the economy must serve people, not the other way around. Work is more than a way to make a living; it is a form of continuing participation in God's creation. If the dignity of work is to be protected, then the basic rights of workers must be respected—the right to productive work, to decent and fair wages, to organize and join unions, to private property, and to economic initiative. Respecting these rights promotes an economy that protects human life, defends human rights, and advances the well-being of all.

Solidarity

Our culture is tempted to turn inward, becoming indifferent and sometimes isolationist in the face of international responsibilities. Catholic social teaching proclaims that we are our brothers' and sisters' keepers, wherever they live. We are one human family, whatever our national, racial, ethnic, economic, and ideological differences. Learning to practice the virtue of solidarity means learning that "loving our neighbor" has global dimensions in an interdependent world. This virtue is described by John Paul II as "a firm and persevering determination to commit oneself to the common good; that is to say to the good of all and of each individual, because we are all really responsible for all" (*Sollicitudo Rei Socialis*, no. 38).

Care for God's Creation

On a planet conflicted over environmental issues, the Catholic Tradition insists that we show our respect for the Creator by our stewardship of creation. Care for the earth is not just an Earth Day slogan, it is a requirement of our faith. We are called to protect people and the planet, living our faith in relationship with all of God's creation. This environmental challenge has fundamental moral and ethical dimensions that cannot be ignored.

This teaching is a complex and nuanced tradition with many other important elements. Principles like "subsidiarity" and the "common good" outline the advantages and limitations of markets, the responsibilities and limits of government, and the essential roles of voluntary associations. These and other key principles are outlined in greater detail in the *Catechism* and in the attached Report of the Content Subgroup (see pp. 32-42). These principles build on the foundation of Catholic social teaching: the dignity of human life. This central Catholic principle requires that we measure every policy, every institution, and every action by whether it protects human life and enhances human dignity, especially for the poor and vulnerable.

These moral values and others outlined in various papal and episcopal documents are part of a systematic moral framework and a precious intellectual heritage that we call Catholic social teaching. The Scriptures say, "Without a vision the people perish" (Prv 29:18). As Catholics, we have an inspiring vision in our social teaching. In a world that hungers for a sense of meaning and moral direction, this teaching offers ethical criteria for action. In a society of rapid change and often confused moral values, this teaching offers consistent moral guidance for the future. For Catholics, this social teaching is a central part of our identity. In the words of John Paul II, it is "genuine doctrine" (*Centesimus Annus*, no. 5).

There will be legitimate differences and debate over how these challenging moral principles are applied in concrete situations. Differing prudential judgments on specifics cannot be allowed, however, to obscure the need for every Catholic to know and apply these principles in family, economic, and community life.

The Educational Challenge

Catholic schools, religious education, adult education, and faith formation programs are vitally important for sharing the substance and values of Catholic social teaching. Just as the social teaching of the Church is integral to Catholic faith, the social justice dimensions of teaching are integral to Catholic education and catechesis. They are an essential part of Catholic identity and formation.

In offering these reflections, we want to encourage a fuller integration of the Church's social tradition into the mainstream of Catholic education and catechesis. We seek to encourage a more integral sharing of the substance of Catholic social teaching in Catholic education and catechesis at every level. The commitment to human life and dignity, to human rights and solidarity, is a calling all Catholic educators must share with their students. It is not a vocation for a few religion teachers, but a challenge for every Catholic educator and catechist.

The Church has the God-given mission and the unique capacity to call people to live with integrity, compassion, responsibility, and concern for others. Our seminaries, colleges, schools, and catechetical programs are called to share not just abstract principles but a moral framework for everyday action. The Church's social teaching offers a guide for choices as parents, workers, consumers, and citizens.

Therefore, we emphasize that the values of the Church's social teaching must not be treated as tangential or optional. They must be a core part of teaching and formation. Without our social teaching, schools, catechetical programs, and other formation programs would be offering an incomplete presentation of our Catholic tradition. This would fall short of our mission and would be a serious loss for those in our educational and catechetical programs.

Directions for the Future

We strongly support new initiatives to integrate the social teachings of the Church more fully into educational and catechetical programs and institutions. Many catechists and Catholic teachers do this every day by weaving these ideas into curricula and classrooms. They introduce their students to issues of social justice. They encourage service to those in need and reflect on the lessons learned in that service. Yet in too many schools and classrooms, these principles are often vaguely presented; the values are unclear; the lessons are unlearned. We support the task force's clear call for new efforts to teach our social tradition and to link service and action, charity and justice.

The report of the task force includes a series of recommendations for making the Church's social teaching more intentional and explicit in all areas of Catholic education and formation. Without summarizing the full agenda, we call attention to several recommendations which we believe deserve priority attention:

Elementary and Secondary Schools

We strongly urge Catholic educators and administrators to create additional resources and programs that will address the lack of familiarity with Catholic social teaching among many faculty and students. We encourage diocesan and local educators to promote curriculum development in the area of Catholic social thought and would like to see a model developed for faculty interested in this arena.

Religious Education, Youth Ministry, and Adult Faith Formation

We support the proposal that diocesan offices (as well as regional and national organizations that work in the areas of religious education, youth ministry, and adult education) focus on Catholic social teaching in meetings and publications. A clearinghouse of existing resources and effective methodologies should be developed, and new resources should be produced. Leadership formation programs should be developed to enhance the explicit teaching of Catholic social doctrine in these educational ministries.

Higher Education

We support the proposal that the Association of Catholic Colleges and Universities and other appropriate national groups explore the creation of a national organization of faculty interested in Catholic social teaching. We support summer seminars for faculty members to examine Catholic teaching and explore ways to incorporate it into classes and programs.

Seminaries and Continuing Formation of Clergy

We also support the recommendation that the United States Catholic Conference (USCC) and the National Catholic Educational Association (NCEA) produce guidelines to aid seminaries in strengthening their teaching of the Church's social doctrine. These guidelines should offer assistance and direction in achieving the goal of having all seminaries require at least one course that is specifically focused on Catholic social teaching. We encourage the suggestion that a symposium be held for seminary instructors involved or interested in teaching Catholic social thought. We urge that diaconate programs incorporate Catholic social teaching fully and explicitly. We further encourage continuing formation of priests so they can more effectively preach, teach, and share the Church's social tradition and its concrete implications for our time.

Textbooks and Catechetical Materials

We call on publishers of Catholic educational materials to continue and to strengthen efforts to incorporate the principles of Catholic social teaching into all materials and disciplines in addition to providing resources specific to Catholic social thought. A standard of assessment for Catholic social teaching, based on the *Catechism of the Catholic Church*, papal teaching, and the documents of our conference, should be developed to assist publishers. The work of the task force can serve as a helpful guide. This review should be coordinated with other assessments for which publishers presently submit their materials. A clearinghouse of lesson plans and other resources should be created to help educators share information and ideas easily.

Conclusion

As bishops and pastors, we believe the Church's social teaching is integral to our identity and mission as Catholics. This is why we seek a renewed commitment to integrate and to share the riches of the Church's social teaching in Catholic education and formation at every level. This is one of the most urgent challenges for the new millennium. As John Paul II has said, "A commitment to justice and peace in a world like ours, marked by so many conflicts and intolerable social and economic inequalities, is a necessary condition for the preparation and celebration of the Jubilee" (*Tertio Millennio Adveniente*, no. 51).

Our conference is committed to following through on the task force report. We urge our Committees on Education, Domestic Social Policy, International Policy, and Priestly Formation and other relevant bodies to continue to bring together more effectively our educational and catechetical ministries and social mission. We encourage other Catholic leaders and educators to read the full report and to develop specific and concrete initiatives flowing from the task force recommendations. We very much welcome the commitment and the initiatives of many national and diocesan organizations to act on these recommendations, developing appropriate structures and programs at the diocesan level, and improving our capacity to teach Catholic social values and make a difference in our world. One promising step at the diocesan level would be bringing together educational and catechetical leaders with those involved in social ministry to form a local task force on this topic to follow through on these recommendations.

The most urgent ecclesial task of our times is the proclamation of the good news of Jesus Christ. A vital element of this new evangelization is sharing our social tradition with all Catholics so clearly that they may be engaged and challenged, encouraged and empowered to live their faith every day. Witnessing to this tradition by the integrity of our own Catholic institutions and organizations is one of the most effective ways to communicate the Church's social teaching.

The test for our Church is not simply have we "kept the faith," but have we shared the faith. As we approach the jubilee of the Lord's birth, we seek to support and to encourage renewed efforts to make the social dimensions of our faith come alive in caring service, creative education, and principled action throughout the Catholic community. Catholic education is one of the most important forums for sharing and demonstrating our Church's commitment to human dignity and social justice. Catholic educators and catechists can best share this message of hope and challenge for the future. We support and encourage them for this holy work.

This is not a new mission. More than two thousand years ago, Jesus in his hometown synagogue read the words from Isaiah that outlined his work on earth, as well as the Church's mission through the centuries and the special tasks of Catholic educators and catechists today:

The Spirit of the Lord is upon me,
   because he has anointed me
      to bring glad tidings to the poor.
. . . liberty to captives
   and recovery of sight to the blind,
      to let the oppressed go free. . . . (Lk 4:18)

Sharing our social tradition more fully and clearly is an essential way to bring good news, liberty, and new sight to a society and world in desperate need of God's justice and peace.

Summary Report

OF THE TASK FORCE ON CATHOLIC SOCIAL TEACHING AND CATHOLIC EDUCATION

January 5, 1998

Introduction

In 1995, the USCC Committees on Education, Domestic Policy, and International Policy established a Task Force on Catholic Social Teaching and Catholic Education. The task force was approved as a "special exception" to the NCCB/USCC Plans and Priorities by the full body of bishops. This initiative reflects the bishops' conviction that the social mission of the Church is central to the overall mission of the Church and integral to the faith of every Catholic. A key to deepening the Catholic community's understanding of this social mission is integrating it fully and effectively in Catholic educational and catechetical programs.

After more than two years of assessment and discussion, the task force agreed that although many Catholic educational and catechetical programs excel in communicating Catholic social thought, there are many others that cover the social mission incompletely, indirectly, or not at all. This situation represents a critical problem for the Church's efforts to hand down the faith accurately and in all its dimensions, as expressed in the *Catechism of the Catholic Church*. It also reveals an urgent need to integrate Catholic social teaching more fully into the Church's educational and catechetical programs. Finally, it creates an opportunity to share our social tradition even more creatively at every level of Catholic education and catechesis.

The bishops charged the Task Force on Catholic Social Teaching and Catholic Education with assessing the extent to which Catholic social thought is now incorporated in Catholic educational and catechetical programs, and with developing recommendations for bringing Catholic social teaching and Catholic education closer together. The task force is composed of leaders in the fields of social ministry, education, and catechesis. The full task force has met six times since November 1995.

The task force has a two-part mandate:

1. To assess the quantity, quality, and content of teaching on Catholic social tradition in our schools and seminaries, our colleges and universities, and our programs of religious education and formation; and

2. To develop and begin to carry forward strategies to deepen, broaden, and strengthen the sharing of Catholic social teaching in our educational institutions and efforts.

To undertake the assessment phase of its work, the task force initially divided into five subgroups: Elementary and Secondary Schools; Religious Education, Youth Ministry, and Adult Education; Higher Education; Seminaries; and Materials. The task force formed a "Content Subgroup" to develop a summary of the key principles of Catholic social teaching that would guide its work. For a period of approximately eighteen months, the subgroups conducted their assessments and developed recommendations for further incorporating Catholic social teaching into their respective educational areas. This process led to a set of preliminary reports presented to the full task force on April 9, 1997.

General Findings

In general, the subgroups determined that there is much interest among Catholic educational, catechetical, and social ministry professionals in incorporating Catholic social teaching into Catholic educational programs. However, the extent to which it actually happens is very uneven and is often lacking depth or clarity. There are varied reasons for this. Among them are (1) the need to see more clearly Catholic social teaching as authentic doctrine and integral to the mission of Catholic education; (2) a lack of familiarity with Catholic social thought among educators and catechists; (3) a need for greater emphasis and coordination on this topic within national professional organizations; and (4) a lack of materials incorporating Catholic social teaching, including syllabi, textbooks, curricula, and lesson plans.

Several observations were common to all the subgroups:

1. There is a general lack of recognition among Catholics that our social tradition includes an explicit body of teaching that is an essential element of the overall Catholic tradition.

2. There is a consistent need for leadership formation in the area of Catholic social teaching for those in seminaries, programs of continuing education for priests, deacon formation, and lay ministry programs, as well as catechist, youth ministry, and teacher training.

3. There is a universal need to be more explicit in teaching the principles of Catholic social thought and in helping people apply and act on those principles. Offering both experiential learning opportunities and training and reflection on Catholic social teaching is essential.

4. There is a need for Catholic educational and catechetical programs not only to continue offering direct service experiences but also to offer opportunities to work for change in the policies and structures that cause injustice.

The task force acknowledges and commends the remarkable growth in providing service opportunities in Catholic education and formation. These efforts provide essential experiences in serving those in need. They also provide an important opportunity to reflect on the demands of Catholic social teaching for transforming structures that leave people in need. The Catholic social mission requires both service and action for justice. Catholic education and catechesis in all its forms must help believers respond to human suffering and change the structures that threaten human life and dignity.

The summaries below include brief descriptions of the assessment report and recommendations of each of the subgroups, along with additional recommendations made during the full task force discussion. The full texts of the subgroup reports are available from the USCC Departments of Education and Social Development and World Peace, which staffed the task force.

Content Subgroup

The Content Subgroup gathered information from existing Catholic documents, drawing particularly from the *Catechism of the Catholic Church* and from the U.S. bishops' statement, *A Century of Catholic Social Teaching*. The report of the Content Subgroup, which summarizes key principles of Catholic social teaching, is attached (see pp. 32-42).

Elementary and Secondary Schools Subgroup

Assessment

The subcommittee relied on three sources for its assessment: (1) its own broad experience of Catholic schools, (2) an informal survey of schools known to subcommittee members, and (3) an *ex post facto* analysis of the Assessment of Catholic Religious Education (ACRE), which is a national assessment of religious education efforts conducted by the National Catholic Educational Association (NCEA). Based on these sources, the subcommittee is confident in asserting that the fullness of Catholic social teaching needs to be conveyed more effectively to students in Catholic elementary and secondary schools.

Recommendations

In order to promote a fuller living out of Catholic social teaching by students and graduates of Catholic elementary and secondary schools, the subcommittee recommends these steps:

1. that (arch)dioceses be encouraged to incorporate Catholic social teaching in (a) standards for in-service training of teachers and (b) curriculum guidelines

2. the development of a resource for assisting dioceses, parishes, and schools that would include (a) programs, models, and materials for faculty education and for incorporating Catholic social teaching into the elementary and secondary curriculum, (b) a model process for cur-

riculum development in Catholic social teaching, including sample out-comes and assessment tools, and (c) suggestions for incorporating the principles of Catholic social teaching into administrative practices at the (arch)diocesan, parish, and school levels

3. that the NCEA be encouraged to revise the questions in the Assess-ment of Catholic Religious Education (ACRE) to reflect explicitly the components of Catholic social teaching

4. that Catholic schools acknowledge Catholic social teaching to be an essential part of their mission

Religious Education, Youth Ministry, and Adult Education Subgroup

Assessment

One critical dimension to be considered in exploring the relationship between these ministries and Catholic social teaching is the essential link-age between such teaching and spirituality.

The life of Christian discipleship demands the promotion of a consistent ethic of life, which represents a seamless garment of complete responsive-ness in faith to the call of the Gospel. The integral linkage between social justice and spirituality points to a community's whole life in Christ, a life rooted in the Paschal Mystery. Living this mystery is a powerful dimension of the spiritual life, one that fosters doing what is right, loving goodness, and walking humbly with our God (cf. Mi 6:8).Religious education, youth ministry, and adult education invite ministerial linkages with Catholic social teaching. The Subgroup for Religious Education, Youth Ministry, and Adult Education initiated two tracks for assessing the extent of these linkages. First, the subgroup developed reports dealing with selected minis-tries. These reports provided a look at a wide variety of topics and a great diversity of ministries, all in relation to the Church's social teaching.

For its second major initiative, the subgroup conducted a limited sur-vey of twenty-nine leaders in the following ministries: parish catechesis, diocesan catechesis, adult catechesis, youth ministry, social action, and diocesan worship offices. The subgroup asked persons active in these ministries to respond to ten questions dealing with Catholic social teaching and the ministry represented. These were among the group's findings:

1. The "dignity of human life" is a consistent theme in most ministries; however, such themes as "compassion for the poor," "fostering a consistent ethic of life, particularly in economic matters," and "fostering equality for all" are themes that need additional emphasis.

2. For the leaders surveyed, the major avenues for promoting Catholic social teaching are mission statements, workshops and in-service training, and collaboration among diocesan offices to incorporate Catholic social teaching in all efforts.

3. While recognizing the positive effects of Catholic social teaching (it fosters greater discernment in the political arena and raises awareness of the faith perspective in civil society), nearly half of the respondents said that Catholic social teaching has a limited effect and needs to be taught more consistently and comprehensively to church leaders and the general Catholic community.

4. Social justice activities and service projects do not always include reflections on Catholic social teaching.

5. Inclusion of Catholic social teaching in sacramental preparation programs depends on the commitment of the DRE and the familiarity of the presenters. It is more likely to occur during confirmation and RCIA programs.

6. While some respondents found diocesan offices and church documents helpful resources for learning more about Catholic social teaching, others found that there is more emphasis on acting on our social teaching than on learning and teaching it.

7. The greatest challenges to the realization of our social mission are (a) the inability of Catholics to recognize social teaching and social action as intrinsic dimensions of their Christian spirituality; (b) the

tendency of the Church to focus insufficiently on teaching Catholic social thought; (c) the fact that Catholic social teaching is often presented as abstract and disconnected from daily life; and (d) the need to incorporate Catholic social thought more universally into liturgies and homilies.

8. Suggestions for incorporating Catholic social teaching more fully into Catholic life include (a) connecting it to spirituality and the heart of the Christian vocation; (b) providing better training for church leaders and adults, especially the many volunteers in our religious education programs; (c) consistently incorporating our social teaching into liturgies and homilies; and (d) strengthening ties to other religious, community, and school groups around issues of common concern.

Recommendations

The Subgroup on Religious Education, Youth Ministry, and Adult Education developed seven key directions for action as well as specific suggestions for implementing them. For the purposes of this summary, we focus on the general directions for action, adding more specific suggestions only where necessary for clarification.

1. Promote systematic research on the relationship between Catholic social teaching and religious education/youth ministry/adult education.

2. Invite a wide range of national educational, pastoral, and social ministry organizations and conference services to focus on Catholic social teaching at their annual meetings and incorporate a concern for justice into meeting activities on an ongoing basis.

3. Promote ongoing integration of Catholic social teaching inclusive of liturgical catechesis in catechetical/educational programs by developing a basic formation component in programs for adults engaged in ministry.

4. Gather available resources relating to Catholic social teaching, and make their availability known through a national clearinghouse center.

5. Encourage the convening of a national convocation on the topic of strengthening communication of Catholic social teaching.

6. Promote the essential linkage between social justice and spirituality through such means as a "think tank" on spirituality and Catholic social teaching, use of the Internet, focus on the consistent life ethic, and the linkages between sacramental theology and Catholic social teaching.

7. Seek an author for an essay to be distributed nationally on the topic of Catholic social teaching and spirituality.

Higher Education Subgroup

Assessment

The subgroup's report began with a review of the relationship between Catholic higher education and the social mission of the Church; next it turned to an examination of previous efforts to organize campus work for justice and peace. It then summarized the results of a survey completed by 113 Catholic institutions of higher education, more than one-half of the Catholic colleges and universities in the country. Almost all of these institutions expressed a commitment to the Church's social mission. Eighty-four identified one or more courses that address Catholic social teaching, although some of these were general courses on ethics or Catholicism. A majority of the schools mentioned community service as a program that reflects a commitment to Catholic social teaching. Other institutions described programs of outreach to the local community. Fifteen schools described service-learning programs where the service experience is an integral part of a course or courses. Finally, ten schools pointed to peace studies or peace and justice studies.

The subgroup found that while there is clear interest in and support for Catholic social teaching among institutions of higher education, it is generally not offered in a systematic way. There appears to be little consistent attention given to incorporating gospel values and Catholic social teaching into general education courses or into departmental majors. Although service experiences are relatively widespread, there are few opportunities to pursue questions of social justice in an ongoing way. The task of convincing faculties that these are intellectually serious matters appears to be an important challenge.

Recommendations

1. Formation of a national organization or network of Catholic college and university faculty interested in education for justice and peace

2. Formation of a board or steering committee to meet regularly with presidents and leaders of Catholic social justice organizations

3. Diocesan convenings of campus leaders and leaders of social action offices

4. Exploration of funding opportunities for campus curricular and program initiatives

5. Creation of an informal clearinghouse on campus programs and new initiatives

6. Annual gatherings of faculty and campus ministers with national social ministry leaders

7. Summer seminars for selected groups of faculty (by discipline, e.g.) to examine Catholic social teaching and how it might be incorporated into classes and programs

8. Facilitation of national and international meetings of students involved in justice and peace programs

9. Use of the *Journal of Peace and Justice Studies*

10. Preparation of a book describing various national Catholic social ministry organizations and their regional and local affiliates

11. Identification of research needs by Catholic social justice groups to be advertised to faculty and students

Seminaries Subgroup

Our assessment of seminaries revealed that while some seminaries require courses on Catholic social teaching, many do not. We recommend that the NCCB make all seminaries aware of the expectations set forth in the *Program of Priestly Formation* and the Vatican's *Guidelines for the Study and Teaching of the Church's Social Doctrine in the Formation of Priests*, and that the appropriate offices provide assistance to seminaries in offering such courses.

Assessment

The task force and the subgroup first reviewed a survey of seminary programs in this area. Attention then turned to collecting syllabi and other information on courses in Catholic social teaching from seminaries across the country. Roughly one-half of the seminaries in the country responded. Just over one-half of the respondents have at least one required course on Catholic social teaching. Less than one-half listed required or elective courses that cover ethics or social justice issues without specifically focusing on Catholic social teaching. The majority of the seminaries that responded indicated that their programs include some kind of social ministry field placement, most of which are social service experiences, and some of which may be described more accurately as pastoral placements.

The results of this survey suggest that while there are many good examples of courses on Catholic social teaching, there is a serious need to ensure that all seminaries include in their curricula required courses on this topic. The minimum expectation should be implementation of the Vatican's *Guidelines for the Study and Teaching of the Church's Social Doctrine in the Formation of Priests*. Those guidelines state:

> With regard to the space to be reserved for social doctrine within the program of studies in centers for ecclesiastical formation . . . it is not enough to deal with it in some optional lessons within philosophy or theology courses. Required and elective courses on this discipline must be included in the programs. (no. 73)

It is absolutely necessary for knowledge about the major social encyclicals to be ensured during formation. These encyclicals must be the subject of special courses and represent required reading material for the students. (no. 73)

The subgroup identified two questions raised by their survey. One is whether the fact that 50 percent of seminaries chose not to respond suggests anything about whether they offer courses in this area. The other is whether one can assume that a single required course on Catholic social teaching means that the seminarians have assimilated this topic sufficiently. Moreover, an effort must be made to ensure not only the understanding of documents but also a corresponding conversion of life. It is desirable that seminarians cultivate a deep spirituality that connects our celebration of the Eucharist with our commitment to justice in the world.

While the overall concern of this subgroup is ministry formation, time constraints narrowed the focus to seminaries. Other areas that should be considered in the future include schools of theology, deacon formation programs, lay ministry formation programs, and programs of continuing education for the clergy.

Recommendations

1. Produce for seminaries a report of the subgroup's work, including a compilation of the best material from the syllabi, an annotated list of textbooks, and recommended reading.

2. Produce standards to aid seminaries in strengthening the teaching of the Church's social doctrine and guidelines for social ministry placements in service, advocacy, and community organizing groups. These norms might include a target date by which all seminaries would have at least one required course specifically on Catholic social teaching. Seminaries should move beyond mere academic presentation of social justice issues to integration of justice principles into the formation program itself.

3. Convene a symposium for seminary instructors who teach courses on Catholic social teaching, perhaps establishing a network of these instructors.

4. Compile a summary of the major recommendations regarding Catholic social teaching from the *Guidelines for the Study and Teaching of the Church's Social Doctrine in the Formation of Priests* and the *Program of Priestly Formation.*

5. Develop clarifications or changes for the next *Program of Priestly Formation.*

Materials Subgroup

Overview

It was the goal of the Materials Subgroup to undertake an examination of how catechetical materials integrate and communicate Catholic social teaching. Given the fact that there are many materials available for adult education, the subgroup decided to focus its attention on how the principles of Catholic social thought are integrated into the standard religious education texts for children and youth. The *Catechism of the Catholic Church*, and particularly the *Protocol* used by the Ad Hoc Committee to Oversee the Use of the Catechism in its reviews for conformity, along with the key principles of Catholic social teaching set forth in the Report of the Content Subgroup, became the standards for measuring the integration of the Church's social doctrine in religious education materials.

Assessment

The subgroup wrote to fifteen publishers of catechetical materials requesting samples of texts for children and youth that demonstrated the integration of Catholic social teaching. They received responses from nine publishers. After reviewing these materials, the subgroup concluded that the most direct and specific focus on Catholic social teaching is found in materials geared to high school students, and that this is done in an authentic and fairly complete way. Materials for elementary and junior high schools incorporated fewer social teaching themes, but all contained a substantial amount of relevant material. The most dominant principles displayed in the elementary and junior high materials include (1) the life and dignity of the human person, (2) human equality, and (3) the call to family, charity, and justice. The primary emphasis at these grade levels is to incorporate major themes of Catholic social teaching into the overall catechesis of the young student. The content is therefore more general and appropriate to the particular age of the student.

A preliminary review of all materials raises the question of whether the Church's social doctrine is explicitly taught as such (as is the case for other areas of doctrine) or whether it is presented with less authority and integrated into texts only through stories and indirect methodological tools.

Recommendations

1. Current efforts by publishers to incorporate Catholic social teaching into their materials need to be affirmed. Publishers should be encouraged to incorporate the principles of Catholic social thought into all disciplines, while providing materials specific to Catholic social thought. This dialogue with publishers should be a part of the annual publishers' meeting convened by the Committee on Education of the USCC.

2. A standard of assessment for Catholic social teaching, based on the *Catechism of the Catholic Church*, needs to be developed to assist publishers. This standard should take into account age-appropriate presentation of the principles of Catholic social teaching. It should be compatible with and correlated to the present review of catechetical materials conducted by the Ad Hoc Committee to Oversee the Use of the Catechism. This assessment of Catholic social teaching should not become yet another separate process of review to which publishers would need to submit their publications.

3. Lesson plans related to the Church's social doctrine should be developed for different grade levels and be made available to schools and parish programs. Sacramental preparation programs need particular attention. A clearinghouse for additional social teaching resources should also be established to help educators easily share information.

General Recommendations

In addition to the recommendations of the subgroups, the full Task Force on Catholic Social Teaching and Catholic Education offers two key recommendations:

1. The Catholic bishops of the United States should issue a brief pastoral statement affirming the importance of integrating Catholic social teaching into Catholic educational programs. The statement could affirm what is already being done. It might also encourage educators and social ministry leaders to carry out this important task of ensuring that the Catholic community grows in its understanding of the social dimensions of our faith. The statement could incorporate as attachments this summary of the task force's reports as well as the Report of the Content Subgroup.

2. Those members of the Task Force on Catholic Social Teaching and Catholic Education who are able to continue their participation have agreed to meet in 1998 to develop a plan for ensuring that their recommendations are carried out. This follow-up effort is likely to require (a) ongoing commitments from the organizations involved in the task force, (b) convening of informal groups of educators and social ministry leaders, (c) the establishment of an institute on Catholic social teaching and Catholic education at a university or other organization, and (d) similar follow-up activities.

Conclusion

The assessment phase of the work of the Task Force on Catholic Social Teaching and Catholic Education established that there is much good will and significant effort aimed at incorporating Catholic social teaching into Catholic education and formation. Task force members who conducted telephone interviews and written surveys with educational, catechetical, and social ministry professionals found a significant openness and desire for help, as well as a need for practical tools.

However, the task force's work also shows that existing efforts are uneven and inconsistent. The principles of Catholic social teaching are too often shared in a vague way or not at all. As a result, too many Catholics do not understand the substance of the Church's social teaching; they are unable to draw on these principles to help shape their actions in private and public life.

The strategies and recommendations identified by the Task Force on Catholic Social Teaching and Catholic Education will be useful only to the extent that they are implemented. While some may not be realizable in the short run, task force members felt it was necessary to identify important strategies, goals, or recommendations even if they take years to accomplish.

Looking to the future, the task force and its subgroups will do their part to follow up and act on appropriate recommendations. Most important, however, they hope their work will spark the creative energies of bishops, priests, religious, lay leaders, teachers, catechetical leaders, and social ministers throughout the Church whose expertise and commitment are essential if the Church's social mission is to become a truly integral and explicit part of its educational and catechetical programs.

Attachment

ON CATHOLIC SOCIAL TEACHING
AND CATHOLIC EDUCATION

Report of the Content Subgroup

Introduction

Our subgroup has sought to develop a brief summary of the substance of Catholic social teaching which may be useful to the other subgroups of our task force as they assess the integration of Catholic social teaching within Catholic education and develop strategies for the future. This report is not a definitive or comprehensive summary of Catholic social teaching. It seeks to offer a very basic outline of the foundations, principles, and key concepts of Catholic social tradition to help the task force in its work.

While there are a variety of commentaries on the Church's social tradition, this summary is drawn directly from the authoritative documents of the universal Church and the statements of the U.S. bishops on Catholic social teaching. This summary is drawn particularly from the *Catechism of the Catholic Church*, and the U.S. bishops' statement, *A Century of Social Teaching*.

The summary offers a guide to the scriptural roots, theological foundations, and basic principles of the Catholic social tradition. It is not a substitute for the original documents or the wide variety of statements and commentaries applying the tradition to particular issues. To offer more concrete assistance in sharing this tradition in educational settings, we refer the reader to the *Apostolic Constitution, Ex Corde Ecclesiae*, the *General Directory for Catechesis*, the *National Catechetical Directory for Catholics of the United States*, and other related documents.

Foundations

Catholic social teaching is rooted in our understanding of human life and human dignity. Because every human being is created in the image and likeness of God and is redeemed by Jesus Christ, we believe in the sanctity of every human life from conception to natural death. Each person has inherent value and dignity, which come from God and are independent of any human accomplishment or quality.

Our experience of the Triune God is also a basis for Catholic social thought. God has revealed himself to us in creation and in redemption. In the act of creating man and woman and establishing their relationship with each other and with him, God reveals our eminently communal and social nature. In the coming of Jesus Christ, we understand the Trinitarian nature of God's own inner life. Jesus reveals God as Father and sends the Holy Spirit as his gift to us to dwell in our hearts and to form us into community. God's nature is communal and social; therefore our nature, created in his image, is communal and social as well. We are communal and social because of the way we have been created and because of the One who has redeemed us. We are all children of God and share in the Lord's call to justice and peace. We cannot call ourselves Catholic unless we hear and heed the Church's teaching to serve those in need, to protect human life and dignity, and to pursue justice and peace.

The Catholic social tradition is deeply rooted in the Scriptures and expressed in Catholic teaching. It constitutes, in the words of John Paul II, "the Church's 'social doctrine.'" This tradition is

- *founded on the life and words of Jesus Christ*, who came "to bring glad tidings to the poor . . . liberty to captives . . . recovery of sight to the blind" (Lk 4:18-19), and who identified himself with "the least of these," the hungry, the homeless, the stranger (cf. Mt 25:45);

- *inspired by the passion for justice of the Hebrew prophets* and the Scripture's call to care for the weak and to "let justice surge like water" (Am 5:24);

- *articulated by the social teaching of our Church*, including papal encyclicals, conciliar documents, and episcopal statements that have explored and expressed the social demands of our faith, especially over the last century. This tradition insists that work for justice and peace and care for the poor and vulnerable are the responsibility of every Christian;

- *shaped by those who have come before us*, by St. John Chrysostom, by St. Augustine, by St. Francis, and by more recent leaders such as Dorothy Day and countless others whose lives and work have been models of the Christian commitment to justice and peace;

- *lived by the People of God*, who seek to build the kingdom of God, to live our faith in the world, and to apply the values of the Scriptures and the teaching of the Church in our own families and parishes, in our work and service and in local communities, the nation, and the world.

Catholic social teaching is both true doctrine and a framework for action. It is not optional or fringe; it is an integral part of the Christian message and Catholic education. Catholic schools, seminaries, religious education programs, and universities or colleges are called to make a serious effort to share the social mission of the Church. This is not a new challenge. It is a theme of the *National Catechetical Directory* and a recurring theme of the new *Catechism*. Sharing our social teaching is integral to the mission of Catholic education in all its forms.

Basic Principles of Catholic Social Teaching

The development of the Catholic social tradition over the past one hundred years has led to a sophisticated body of teaching that cannot be simplified or summarized easily. However, several key principles have been identified in recent Vatican and episcopal documents. The principles listed below are drawn primarily from the new *Catechism of the Catholic Church* and the U.S. bishops' 1991 statement, *A Century of Social Teaching*.

The Life and Dignity of the Human Person

In the Catholic social tradition, the human person is central. Every human life has inherent value and dignity, independent of race, gender, age, or economic status. Because we believe in the inherent value and dignity of every life, we believe the test of every institution or policy is whether it enhances or threatens human life and human dignity. In the Catholic tradition, people are more important than things.

Human Equality

Equality of all persons comes from their essential dignity, having been created in God's image and likeness. While differences in talents are a part of God's plan, social and cultural discrimination in fundamental rights on the basis of sex, race, color, social conditions, language, or religion are not compatible with God's design. Excessive economic and social disparities are contrary to the virtues of social justice, human dignity, and peace.

The Rights and Responsibilities of the Human Person

Each person, reflecting their God-given dignity, has basic rights and responsibilities that flow from our human nature and belong to us as humans regardless of any social or political structures. These rights begin with the right to life. They include those things that make life truly human, such as the rights to freedom of conscience and worship; to raise a family; to immigrate; to live without discrimination; and to have a share of earthly goods sufficient for oneself and one's family, including adequate food, clothing, housing, health care, education, employment, and a safe environment. These rights carry corresponding responsibilities—to one another, to our families, to our communities, and to the larger society—to respect the rights of others and to work for the common good.

The Call to Family

Every human being is intrinsically social, finding fulfillment in relationship to God and other persons, and realizing our dignity and rights in relationship with others, in our families and in our communities. No relationship is more central than the family. It is where we learn about moral principles and where we learn to act on them. The state and all other institutions have an obligation to respect the family and to foster and protect it, not to undermine it.

The Call to Community and Participation

Because of our social nature, all human beings have a right and a responsibility to participate in society and in the institutions that make up our communities. These institutions have important roles in protecting the life, the dignity, and the rights of the person; promoting economic initiative and the well-being of our families and communities; and pursuing the common good. A central moral test of political, legal, and economic institutions is what they do *to* people, what they do *for* people, and how people might *participate* in them. The right to participate in society must be promoted and protected by the state and other institutions. With the *right* to participate comes an *obligation* to participate in the life of the community and in the structures that shape public life. We have a responsibility to exercise our right to participate in a fair and equitable way for the good of all.

The Dignity of Work and the Rights of Workers

In Catholic thought, work is more than a way to make a living; it is a way of expressing and realizing our dignity, and it is an opportunity to collaborate with God in the development of creation. Therefore, workers should participate in the workplace in a manner reflecting their responsibilities and dignity. Employers should treat workers with respect; they cannot be reduced to mere commodities. People have the right to productive work, to fair wages, and to private property and economic initiative. The Church has a long tradition of supporting workers' rights to form and join unions and worker associations of their choosing. In Catholic teaching, the economy exists to serve people, not the other way around.

The Option for the Poor and Vulnerable

Poor and vulnerable people have a special place in the Catholic tradition that is reflected in the challenge of the Hebrew prophets, in Jesus' parable of the Last Judgment (Mt 25:31-46), and in many papal and episcopal social documents of the past one hundred years. The Church appeals to everyone to recognize a special obligation to the poor and vulnerable to defend and to promote their dignity and to ensure that they can participate fully in society. A basic moral test of a society is how its most vulnerable members are faring. This is not promotion of "class struggle" nor an exclusive preference. It reflects the principle of solidarity and our call as Christians to respond to the needs of *all* of our brothers and sisters, *especially* those with the greatest needs. We do this through acts of charity, through meeting the immediate material needs of those who are poor and vulnerable, as well as through our own participation in society, shaping political and economic institutions that meet basic needs, promote justice, and ensure the participation of all.

Solidarity

Solidarity expresses the Catholic image of the *Mystical Body,* that we are one human family, regardless of our national, racial, ethnic, economic, and ideological differences. It calls us to see others not as "enemy" but as "neighbor," and it requires a just social order where goods are fairly distributed and the dignity of all is respected. As our world grows more and more interdependent, these responsibilities cross national and regional boundaries. Violent conflict, poverty, and the denial of dignity and rights to people anywhere on the globe diminish each of us. The principle of solidarity calls us to work for world peace, global development, protection of the environment, and international human rights.

Subsidiarity

Because of our interdependence as expressed by the principle of solidarity, the Church supports the development of voluntary associations and institutions at the local, national, and international levels to promote development in such areas as economic and social life, cultural and recreational activities, professional pursuits, and political affairs. These institutions have important roles as well as limitations. The principle of subsidiarity defends the freedom of initiative of every member of society—and of the intermediate institutions that make up society—from excessive intervention by the state or other larger institutions. The Church vigorously defends the unique roles of families, community associations, and other intermediate institutions and insists their roles cannot be ignored or absorbed by the state or other large institutions. However, when the common good or the rights of individuals are harmed or threatened, society—including governmental institutions—has a responsibility to act to protect human dignity and rights.

The Common Good

The common good is understood as the social conditions that allow people to reach their full human potential and to realize their human dignity. The common good has three essential elements:

1. *Respect for the person,* reflected in social structures that promote each person's opportunity to realize his or her human dignity

2. *The social well-being and development of the group,* reflected in social structures that promote development and make accessible what is necessary for a truly human life, including food, clothing, health, work, education and culture, a safe environment, and the right to establish a family

3. *Peace and security,* protected by the public authority to ensure a just order

In an age of global interdependence, the Church recognizes a *universal common good* and affirms the need for international structures that can promote the just development of the human family across regional and national lines.

The Universal Destination of Goods, the Right to Private Property, and the Integrity of Creation

The goods of this world are intended by God for the benefit of everyone. Therefore, there is a universal purpose of all created goods that exist to promote the right to life and the dignity of all. We are called to see a "social mortgage" that guides our use of the world's goods, and we are invited to be "social trustees" of the goods of the world for today and for the future.

Private property is the necessary means for the maintenance and success of self and family. Therefore, each person has a right to private property. But this right is not absolute. The ownership of property carries a responsibility to use it in ways that are consistent with the common good. Moreover, political authorities have the duty to regulate the exercise of the right to private property for the purpose of promoting the common good.

Use of the resources of the universe cannot be separated from respect for the integrity of creation and a commitment to its preservation. Respect for the Creator is demonstrated by our care for creation. Our commitment to the common good and our concern for our neighbors and for generations yet to come require responsible stewardship of the earth.

Economic Initiative

All people have the right to economic initiative, to use their talents to contribute to the common good and to reap the just fruits of their labor. The state has an obligation to regulate the pursuit of economic initiative for the sake of the common good, but it should not unnecessarily interfere with the individual's opportunity for creative enterprise.

Charity and Justice

From the Hebrew prophets to Christ's description of the Last Judgment, the Scriptures are clear that we are called to help those in need and to oppose unjust and oppressive laws. The practice of charity and the pursuit of justice are linked and complementary duties. The principle of the *preferential option for the poor and vulnerable* demands that we respond to the needs of others and work to ensure their full participation in economic and political life. The tradition of the *corporal works of mercy* calls us to provide direct aid to those in need, offering food for the hungry, providing shelter for the homeless, clothing the naked, visiting the sick and imprisoned, and burying the dead. While these charitable acts are essential, they are not a sufficient response to the Christian vocation. We are also called to work for justice. In our daily lives, through our roles at work, in our communities, in our families, and as citizens, we are called to participate in shaping a social order that promotes just relationships and safeguards human rights.

Call to Action

These principles and concepts are not just abstract theory and ideas, they are a framework for action. They compel believers to these actions:

- *Protecting human life* from conception to natural death and resisting the violence of abortion, the vengeance of capital punishment, the despair of euthanasia and assisted suicide. We believe every life is sacred no matter how young or how old, whatever the race, ethnicity, nationality, or physical condition of each person.

- *Promoting economic justice* and measuring society by how the poor and vulnerable are faring, by how the dignity of work and the rights of workers are respected, and by the practice of the virtue of solidarity in local, national, and global policies.

- *Pursuing peace* in a world marked by too much violence and too little development. Catholic teaching offers a moral framework for interdependence and ethical criteria for the use of force in defense of human life and dignity.

- *Caring for creation* as a sign of respect for the Creator. An authentic environmental ethic is an expression of stewardship for the creation God has given us.

In our efforts to protect "the least among us," to promote the common good, and to pursue justice and peace, it is vital that believers share the principles of Catholic social teaching and act on our faith in the marketplace, the public square, family life, and all community life. As the Second Vatican Council has taught and as John Paul II has repeatedly pointed out, the laity has a preeminent role in working for justice and peace in every aspect of society—as parents, workers, educators, consumers, businesspeople, citizens, and taxpayers. Christians are called by the Scriptures to be the salt, light, and leaven in human society.

Conclusion

These principles, concepts, and applications can provide a general framework for assessment and action by Catholic educators. Catholic educational ministries and institutions can review curricula and programs for how the spirit and substance of the Catholic social tradition are reflected in their educational activities: Are they integral or optional? Are the central ideas taught or assumed? Is the Church's concern for human life and dignity, justice and peace integrated clearly into the curriculum and life of the school, seminary, religious education program, college, or university?

Sources

There are many valuable sources of information on Catholic social teaching from all over the world. A complete survey of these documents is beyond the scope of this report. We have focused our work on Vatican and U.S. documents on social justice and Catholic education. The following have served as the principal sources for the work of the Task Force on Catholic Social Teaching and Catholic Education.

Papal, Conciliar, and Synodal Documents on Social Justice

- *Centesimus Annus (On the Hundredth Anniversary of Rerum Novarum)*
- *Evangelium Vitae (The Gospel of Life)*
- *Familiaris Consortio (On the Family)*
- *Gaudium et Spes (Constitution on the Church in the Modern World)*
- *Justice in the World*
- *Laborem Exercens (On Human Work)*
- *Mater et Magistra (On Christianity and Social Progress)*
- *Octogesima Adveniens (On the Occasion of the Eightieth Anniversary of the Encyclical Rerum Novarum)*
- *Pacem in Terris (Peace on Earth)*
- *Populorum Progressio (On the Development of Peoples)*
- *Quadragesimo Anno (On Reconstructing the Social Order)*
- *Redemptor Hominis (Redeemer of Man)*
- *Rerum Novarum (On the Condition of Workers)*
- *Sollicitudo Rei Socialis (On Social Concern)*
- *Deus Caritas Est (God Is Love)**
- *Spe Salvi (On Christian Hope)**

Papal, Conciliar, and Synodal Documents on Education

- *Catechism of the Catholic Church*
- *Ex Corde Ecclesiae (On Catholic Universities)*
- *General Directory for Catechesis*
- *Guidelines for the Study and Teaching of the Church's Social Doctrine in the Formation of Priests*

U.S. Episcopal Documents on Social Justice

- *A Century of Social Teaching* (out of print)
- *The Challenge of Peace*
- *Communities of Salt and Light*
- *Economic Justice for All*
- *The Harvest of Justice Is Sown in Peace*
- *Program of Social Reconstruction*
- *Putting Children and Families First*
- *Renewing the Earth*
- *Brothers and Sisters to Us/Nuestros Hermanos Y Hermanas* *

U.S. Episcopal Documents on Education

- *National Catechetical Directory for Catholics of the United States*
- *To Teach as Jesus Did*

Other

- *Compendium of the Social Doctrine of the Church* *

---

* These documents were added to the list at the time of the 2009 revised edition.

Resources Available
from the United States Conference
of Catholic Bishops

Titles are in alphabetical order.

Brothers and Sisters to Us/Nuestros Hermanos Y Hermanas
This is the landmark pastoral letter from the bishops in which they promote discussion and action against racism, "an evil which endures in our society and in our Church."
No. 653-0, 32 pp.

Catholic Framework for Economic Life
Ten points from the bishops are presented in two convenient formats for distribution and display.
Card:
English: No. 5-139
Spanish: No. 5-140
Poster:
English: No. 5-137
Spanish: No. 5-138

Charity in Truth (*Caritas in Veritate*)
Pope Benedict XVI shares his thoughts on social justice. In his third encycylical, the Holy Father reminds us of the importance of recognizing the social and economic needs of all people. He affirms that the efforts to improve the condition of humanity must continue.
No. 7-049, 100 pp.

Communities of Salt and Light
Reflections on the Social Mission of the Parish
This bishops' statement presents seven elements of the social mission of parishes as a framework for planning and assessing that ministry.
No. 5-764, 32 pp.

Credible Signs of Christ Alive (by John P. Hogan)
These six case studies from the Catholic Campaign for Human Development include discussion questions, suggested parish action, related contacts, and options for further study.
No. 3167-8, 144 pp.

General Directory for Catechesis
An essential companion to the *Catechism of the Catholic Church*, the *General Directory for Catechesis* (GDC) provides religious educators, teachers, and catechists with a single point of reference for all aspects of catechetical instruction, for content and pedagogy, as well as for methodology. Beginning with an introductory reflection of how contemporary human and ecclesial conditions have impacted the preaching of the Gospel, the GDC moves through a detailed presentation of the goals and essential elements of catechesis, from its role in the Church's mission of evangelization, to norms and guidelines for its presentation, to adaptations for various groups and situations.
English: No. 5-225, 300 pp.
Spanish: No. 5-226, 300 pp.

God Is Love (*Deus Caritas Est*)
In today's high-tech, fast-paced world, love is often portrayed as being separate from Church teaching. With his first encyclical, Pope Benedict XVI hopes to overturn that perception and describe the essential place of love in the life of the Church. The Holy Father explains the various dimensions of love, highlighting the distinctions between "eros" and "agape," Jesus as the incarnate love of God, and the scriptural law of love. In part two, he links the Church's charitable work with the love of God as Trinity, noting that the Church

must express love through acts of justice and charity. This encyclical is an ideal reflection for religious and civic leaders, those preparing for marriage, and those engaged in justice and charitable work.
English: No. 5-758, 64 pp.
Spanish: No. 5-922, 64 pp.

The Gospel of Life (*Evangelium Vitae*)
On the Value and Inviolability of Human Life
Reaffirming the "greatness and inestimable value of human life," in this encyclical letter Pope John Paul II discusses the present-day legal, ethical, and moral threats to life.
English: No. 316-7, 196 pp.
Spanish: No. 317-5, 196 pp.

The Harvest of Justice Is Sown in Peace
A Reflection of the National Conference of Catholic Bishops on the Tenth Anniversary of "The Challenge of Peace"
The bishops confront the trend to isolationism in U.S. foreign policy and acknowledge the importance of nonviolence. The document addresses the just-war theory, humanitarian intervention, deterrence, conscientious objection, and the development of people.
No. 705-7, 28 pp.

Leader's Guide to *Sharing Catholic Social Teaching*
A companion to the bishops' reflection on the central role of Catholic social teaching in the life of the Church, this Leader's Guide provides a flexible resource for infusing Catholic social teaching into a variety of programs and activities. In three easy-to-follow sessions, the guide helps familiarize leaders with Catholic social teaching; helps them integrate those teachings into formational activities; and engages children, youth, and adults to act on the teaching in both charitable service and action for justice. Designed for religious educators at the diocesan and parish levels.
No. 5-366. 64 pp.

On Christian Hope (*Spe Salvi*)

In his encyclical letter *On Christian Hope*, Pope Benedict XVI elaborates the significance of Christian hope in eternal life for contemporary Catholics by presenting examples of hope from the New Testament and saints of the Church. After affirming the modern practice of working to progress in faith with the help of reason, he reminds readers that hope ultimately depends on trusting in God's love for us, and that Christians can be strengthened by turning to God together, in community.
English: No. 7-039, 64 pp.
Spanish: No. 7-804, 64 pp.

On the Family (*Familiaris Consortio*)

Pope John Paul II's apostolic exhortation addresses the role of the family in society as a believing and evangelizing community, in dialogue with God and at the service of all people.
No. 833-9, 93 pp.

On Human Work (*Laborem Exercens*)

Pope John Paul II focuses on "the dignity and rights of those who work." Drawing on biblical teaching and Catholic social thought, he discusses just remuneration for work, the rights of labor unions, the rights and responsibility of management, roles of women, multinational corporations, disabled workers, and other labor questions.
No. 825-8, 62 pp.

On Social Concern (*Sollicitudo Rei Socialis*)

Pope John Paul II's encyclical letter commemorates the twentieth anniversary of Pope Paul VI's *Populorum Progressio* and reaffirms the continuity of the Church's teaching on social doctrine.
No. 205-5, 104 pp.

Peace on Earth (*Pacem in Terris*)

Pope John XXIII's landmark encyclical letter promotes universal peace in truth, justice, charity, and liberty.
No. 5-602, 56 pp.

Putting Children and Families First
A Challenge for Our Church, Nation, and World
The bishops stress the need for national policy decisions that address protecting the lives of children, economic help for families, helping families at work, families and discrimination, meeting children's basic needs, divorce and child support, and broader cultural forces.
No. 469-4, 24 pp.

Renewing the Earth
An Invitation to Reflection and Action on Environment in Light of Catholic Social Teaching
The bishops call on Catholics to reflect on and to discuss environmental problems, including global warming; depletion of the ozone layer; deforestation; and toxic and nuclear waste.
No. 468-6, 20 pp.

Tenth Anniversary Edition of *Economic Justice for All*
Catholic Social Teaching and the U.S. Economy
Includes the follow-up document *A Decade After Economic Justice for All* as well as *A Catholic Framework for Economic Life* approved by the bishops in November 1996. The bishops urge individuals and institutions to work for a greater justice based on Scripture, church teaching, and ethical norms.
No. 5-135, 160 pp.

Themes from Catholic Social Teaching
Cards and posters explaining the seven themes of Catholic social teaching.
Card:
English: No. 5-315P
Spanish: No. 5-815P
Poster:
English: No. 5-318
Spanish: No. 5-818

To Teach as Jesus Did
A Pastoral Message on Catholic Education
The bishops discuss educational ministry to people of all ages and encourage planning and collaboration in developing educational programs. The publication includes study questions.
No. 063-X, 58 pp.